My Religion and Me
We are
Jews

Philip Blake

W

FRANKLIN WATTS
LONDON•SYDNEY

First published in 2008 by Franklin Watts

Franklin Watts
338 Euston Road
London, NW1 3BH

Franklin Watts Australia
Level 17/207 Kent Street
Sydney, NSW 2000

Copyright © Franklin Watts 2008

Series designed and created for Franklin Watts by Storeybooks.

Acknowledgements
The Publisher would like to thank Kelly Heyman, Yosef Lachman, Leah Linfield and
Saul Montagu.
We would also like to thank the Oxford Synagogue and Jewish Centre for their help.
Faith advisor: Jonathan Gorsky, Heythrop College, University of London

Photo credits: iStockphoto pp 1, 2, 15, 19, 20, 21, 30 and 31; Tudor Photography pp
1, 3, 6, and 12-17.

Additional photographs were supplied by the children featured in the book.
Every attempt has been made to clear copyright. Should there be any inadvertent
omission please apply to the publisher for rectification.

Dewey number: 296

ISBN: 978 0 7496 8017 6

Printed in China

Franklin Watts is a division of Hachette Children's Books,
an Hachette Livre UK company.
www.hachettelivre.co.uk

Note:
The opinions expressed in this book are personal to the children
we talked to and all opinions are subjective and can vary.

Due to the nature of the Jewish faith, the photographs in this book,
including those depicting the Sabbath, were posed and were not
taken on the Sabbath.

Contents

Words in **bold** can be found in the glossary.

What is Judaism?

Judaism is the religion of the Jewish people. The Jews trace their ancestry back many centuries to Abraham, who probably lived about 3,500 years ago and who settled in the land of Canaan (now known as Israel) in the eastern Mediterranean.

One God

Jews believe in one God. Every day they **recite** the Shema, a passage of **scripture** that begins, "Hear O Israel, the Lord our God, the Lord is One". God is both the creator of the universe and the source of everything that is good and loving in the world. He is such a holy being that many Jews believe that his name is too sacred to pass human lips.

▲ Jerusalem became the most important city for the Jews when King David made it his **capital** about 3,000 years ago.

▼ People pray at the Western Wall, the only remaining part of the **Second Temple** in Jerusalem.

A way of life

The Jews believe that about 3,200 years ago God appeared to the Jewish leader Moses, and revealed to him His wishes for His people. He gave Moses the **Torah**, the first five books of the **Hebrew** Bible, which contains all the commandments Jews must obey. When Jews worship in the **synagogue**, part of the Torah is read out loud. Reading God's commandments reminds Jews that God is always present everywhere and that they must obey him all the time, in every part of their lives.

Anyone born to a Jewish mother is Jewish. But for many, being a Jew means much more than who your parents are. It means following the religion of the Jews and obeying God's commandments to his people as laid down in the Torah.

▲ *Reading the Torah at the synagogue.*

◀ *Leah and her family live in Florida, in the USA. The family is at the heart of Jewish life and Jewish families celebrate **festivals** and honour religious traditions together.*

Judaism Around the World

Over the centuries, Jews have travelled widely from their homeland in Israel. There are now Jews living in many different parts of the world.

Forced to move

In ancient times, the Jewish homeland, the land of Israel, was frequently invaded by other peoples. Many Jews were forced to leave and gradually settled in other countries. Jews often made a big contribution to their new countries, but even in modern times they sometimes experienced great suffering and had to leave their homes and go and live elsewhere.

Today there are about 13 million Jews. The largest Jewish communities are in Israel and the United States and there are smaller communities in many parts of the world.

My name is Leah. I live in Florida in the USA. I am eight years old and the sixth of seven children. Because my family is so large, it means there is always someone to play with – my house can be noisy! I go to a Jewish school, where we learn general studies for half of the day and Jewish studies for the other half. Each week, I visit sick people in the hospital. We call this Bikur Cholim.

My name is Saul and I live with my mother in Oxford, England. I am eight years old and go to St Ebbe's Primary School in Oxford. I have lots of friends there. My favourite subject is history. I like playing with our rescue dog Shandy. My hobbies include ice-skating and trampolining.

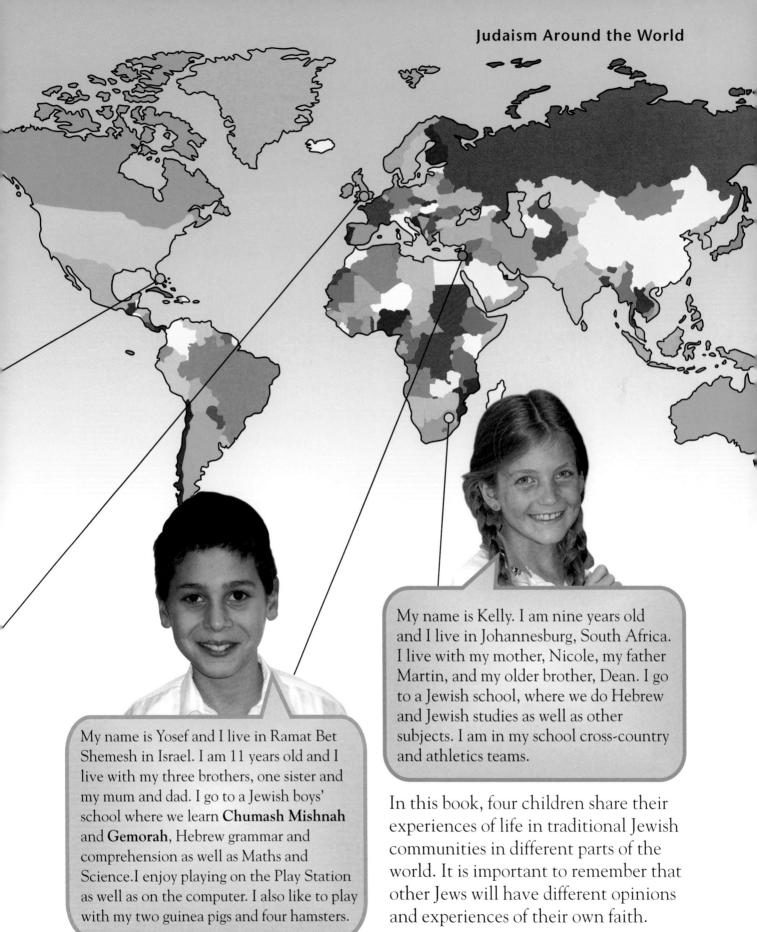

My name is Kelly. I am nine years old and I live in Johannesburg, South Africa. I live with my mother, Nicole, my father Martin, and my older brother, Dean. I go to a Jewish school, where we do Hebrew and Jewish studies as well as other subjects. I am in my school cross-country and athletics teams.

My name is Yosef and I live in Ramat Bet Shemesh in Israel. I am 11 years old and I live with my three brothers, one sister and my mum and dad. I go to a Jewish boys' school where we learn **Chumash Mishnah** and **Gemorah**, Hebrew grammar and comprehension as well as Maths and Science. I enjoy playing on the Play Station as well as on the computer. I also like to play with my two guinea pigs and four hamsters.

In this book, four children share their experiences of life in traditional Jewish communities in different parts of the world. It is important to remember that other Jews will have different opinions and experiences of their own faith.

A Jewish Life
Yosef's story

▲ *I wash my hands using the Kayli.*

When I wake up I say my prayers and wash my hands with a Kayli, a special cup with two handles. As I do this, I say a blessing and a prayer to thank G-d that I have come back to life after being asleep.

Getting dressed

When I get dressed I put on a tzitzit. This is a four-cornered garment with strings on each corner; the eight strings are tied into four knots. I always wear my small cap, called a **kippah**. It reminds me that G-d is always above me, and shows that we **revere** him.

Because some Jewish people believe that the God's name is too holy to spell out or say out loud, some Jews use the form G-d, while others say HaShem, the Hebrew words for 'the name'.

Leah says:
During morning prayers I praise God and ask Him to help me be a good person.

On the doorposts

Every doorway in our house (except for the ones to the kitchen and toilets) has a mezuzah, a narrow container that holds a piece of **parchment**. The Shema is written on the parchment. This is the verse of scripture that we say every day. We put it there because G-d ordered the Jewish people to write these verses on the doorposts of our houses.

▲ *I touch the mezuzah as I enter the room.*

Saul says:

The scroll that is kept inside the mezuzah reminds us of God whenever we go in or out of the door.

Festivals

The Jewish year has many festivals and holy days (see pages 30–31). At these times our house looks very different. For example, at **Sukkot** we build a Sukkah, which is a little house, outside. This reminds us of how the Jews had to put up little houses like this when they travelled from Egypt to their homeland, thousands of years ago. We decorate our Sukkah and have our meals there – some people even sleep in their Sukkah for the week of the festival.

◀ *Reading the Hebrew Bible is very important.*

Shabbat

Yosef's story

▲ *My mother lights the Shabbat candles.*

Saul says:
On Shabbat we must not use electricity, so we play games such as chess or board games instead of watching TV.

Shabbat is the Jewish day of rest. We rest on this day because G-d created the world in six days and rested on the seventh. Shabbat begins on Friday evening and ends on Saturday evening. At Shabbat we are not allowed to do any work at all. This means that we must not cook, drive, use a computer, or even turn on the lights in our house. At Shabbat the whole family gets together. We have a special meal and my father and big brothers go to the synagogue.

Songs for Shabbat

Before my father and brothers go to the synagogue, my mother lights candles. When they get back we all sing the song, Shalom Aleichem (Peace Unto You), which welcomes in the Shabbat. We also sing another song, Eishes Chayil (A Woman of Valour), a song in honour of Jewish women, for my mother.

Preparing for the meal

My father then makes Kiddush (the special Shabbat prayer that is said over a cup of wine) and he blesses us children. We wash our hands and say a bracha (blessing) and my father slices the two loaves of challa, a kind of bread that we eat on Shabbat, and gives us each a slice.

▲ Father blesses me before the meal.

◀ Wine and challa on the Shabbat table.

The Shabbat meals

I look forward to the Shabbat meal because we always have special foods. On Friday night we eat fish and salads to start, chicken soup with kneidelech (**matzah** balls), chicken with potatoes, and finally dessert. For lunch on Saturday, we have cholent (a kind of stew), kugel (a pudding of potatoes or noodles) and cold meats.

Kelly says:

On Friday evening I usually go to the children's service at the synagogue. They give prizes for the best girl and boy davener (prayer), and sometimes I win.

▲ At the end of the Shabbat we make Havdalah, saying blessings over wine, sweet-smelling spices and a special candle flame.

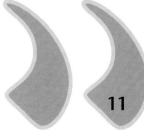

11

At my Synagogue
Saul's story

▲ *The Torah scrolls are kept in the Ark.*

My synagogue is a big building. There's plenty of room for all the men to sit at the front and the women to sit at the back. Right at the front is the Ark, a big cupboard where the Torah scrolls are kept. In the middle is the Bimah, a raised platform where the Torah is read.

Words on the walls

The Ten Commandments are written in Hebrew on the walls. There is also the Hebrew sentence, "Da lifnei mi atah omed". This means, "Know who you are standing before", in other words, remember that you are standing in front of God. I think these words are really important because they remind us of God's presence and of what He wants us to do both in the synagogue and throughout the whole universe.

Children's blessing

At the end of the service there is a special children's blessing. We all go up on the Bimah. The adults hold a prayer shawl over our heads and say a blessing, "God bless you and look after you".

Learning Hebrew

On Sundays, I go to classes at the synagogue to learn Hebrew. I began by learning the alef-bet, the Hebrew alphabet, which is written very differently from the letters we use in English. Then the teacher taught me lots of Hebrew words, so that I can read the prayers.

Building and people

A synagogue is a building where a group of people gather together to pray and worship God. For a service to take place, ten or more people (usually ten men or boys over thirteen years, but ten adults in some synagogues) have to be present. This number is called a minyan.

Leah says:
I learn Hebrew every day at my school, so there is no need for me to have separate Hebrew classes at the synagogue.

▲ *The six-pointed Star of David, named after the great Jewish king David, has been a symbol of Judaism for hundreds of years. It is displayed on the synagogue gates.*

▼ *We learn to recognise the Hebrew letters.*

At Prayer
Saul's story

At home I pray every day when I get up and when I go to bed. Once a week I go to the synagogue and I join in the prayers there. I think it's important to pray, because God is with us for every moment of our lives and it would be rude not to talk to Him.

Ways to pray
Sometimes I pray quietly, sometimes out loud. When we pray out loud, we sing the words of our prayers, and I especially like the special tunes we use for these prayers.

▲ *I wear my kippah to pray and I cover my eyes to say the Shema.*

We have lots of Jewish books at home. ▶

Yosef says:
I say a bracha (blessing) when I wash my hands in the morning and when I sit down to eat a meal.

Leah says:
When we pray we face in the direction of Jerusalem. In the United States that means facing East.

The Shema

One of the most important parts of the Torah is the passage called the Shema. It tells us that God is one being, that we should love Him, and that we should recite these words often.

Covering the head

Boys and men cover their heads when they pray. Like most Jewish boys, I cover my head with a cap called a kippah. I do this to show respect to God.

Tallit and tefillin

When I'm older I will wear a prayer shawl, called a tallit, together with tefillin when I pray at the synagogue. The tallit has little strings on the corner. The strings are tied in a special way and when we say the Shema, we kiss them. Tefillin are little boxes containing small scrolls with the Shema written on them.

Kelly says:
We have prayers at school every morning. When I say the Shema I sometimes pray that I can get a dog for a pet.

The Shema

Hear, O Israel, the Lord our God, the Lord is One. You shall love the Lord your God with all your heart, with all your soul and with all your might. These words which I command you this day you shall take to heart. You shall teach them **diligently** to your children. You shall recite them when you are at home and when you are away, morning and night. You shall bind them as a sign on your hand, they shall be a reminder above your eyes, and you shall **inscribe** them on the doorposts of your home and on your gates.

▲ *Tefillin have leather straps. The wearer winds these around his arm and head.*

The Torah
Saul's story

▲ *I watch the rabbi as he reads the Torah.*

The Torah is the most important Jewish scripture. Its name means "teaching" and it is special because its words are the words that God himself revealed to the Jewish leader, Moses, about 3,200 years ago.

Stories and commandments

I like to hear the stories in the Torah of the first Jewish people, such as Abraham, Jacob and Moses. The Torah also contains all the commandments that God gave to Moses. So it's important that we read the Torah to understand how God wants us to behave.

The Torah scrolls

In the synagogue, the Torah, written on large scrolls, is kept in the Ark. When the Torah is taken out of the Ark, everyone stands up to show their respect. There is an embroidered cloth cover over the scrolls. The cover protects the scrolls and makes them look beautiful. On the scrolls, the words of the Torah are written in Hebrew by hand. Only a Hebrew **scribe**, who is specially trained to use a quill pen and ink, may make a new copy of the text.

Reading the scrolls

When I am older I will be allowed to read from the Torah scrolls, so I watch what the readers do very carefully. The reader follows the text using a pointer called a yad – he does not touch the parchment with his hand because if he did so, he might damage the scroll.

▲ *The Torah is written on a scroll made of parchment.*

Leah says:
The Torah contains God's instructions to His people. It tells us how to lead a **meaningful**, holy life.

Yosef says:
We read from the Torah every Monday, Thursday, on Shabbat as well as on Jewish festivals.

◀ *Beautiful cloth covers protect the Torah scrolls.*

Jewish Food
Leah's story

T he Torah book of Vayikra (called Leviticus in English) includes lots of rules about the kinds of foods Jewish people are allowed to eat and the way food is prepared. Although there are quite a few foods I'm not allowed to eat, there are still plenty of dishes I really enjoy.

Kosher foods

The foods that Jewish people are allowed to eat are called kosher. Meat from animals that have split hooves and **chew the cud**, such as cows or sheep, is kosher, as long as the animals have been **slaughtered** in the correct way. Some birds, such as chicken and turkey, and fish that have fins and scales, are kosher, too. Pork, shellfish and birds that eat other birds are treif, or **forbidden**.

▲ My sisters and I are making chicken schnitzel in my family's kitchen.

Saul says:
One of my favourite foods is matzah. It is a kind of cracker-like bread that we eat instead of ordinary bread at the festival of Pesach (Passover).

Favourite foods

My favourite foods are cheese and vegetable pizza, and chicken and turkey. I really like the dairy foods, such as cheesecake, that we eat on Shavuot, the holiday that **commemorates** the giving of the Torah. I also like the custom of eating apples dipped in honey for a sweet New Year.

▲ *Apples and honey are favourite New Year foods.*

A kosher kitchen

My mother has a kosher kitchen. This means that she prepares foods in the correct way, storing and preparing meat and dairy foods separately. Because meat and dairy should never be mixed, she uses one part of the kitchen for preparing meat and one part for dairy products. She also has separate dishes, plates and cutlery for meat and dairy foods.

▲ *The kitchen has separate sides for preparing meat and dairy foods.*

◄ *Each place setting has a "bencher", a book containing blessings and songs used at mealtimes and on holidays.*

The Holiest Day
Kelly's story

▲ This picture of me was taken at my school, where I learned all about the High Holy days, such as Yom Kippur.

▼ This rabbi is blowing the shofar.

Coming after New Year, Yom Kippur is the most solemn and holy day in the Jewish year. It is the Day of Atonement, on which Jewish people ask for forgiveness for their sins.

A day of prayer

After New Year we spend ten days saying sorry for all our sins. At the end of this time comes Yom Kippur itself, when we ask for forgiveness. We spend most of the day praying at the synagogue. When the end of Yom Kippur comes, the rabbi blows a very long blast on the shofar, a musical instrument made from a ram's horn.

Fasting

On Yom Kippur, adults have nothing to eat or drink from sunset to sunset the next day as a way of showing that they are sorry for their sins. Boys under the age of Bar Mitzvah (13) and girls below the age of Bat Mitzvah (12) (see page 26) do not have to fast all day, but I try to fast for as long as I can – and I never have any sweets or treats on this day.

Giving to charity

At this time of year we give money to charity, which is also a way of asking forgiveness for our sins. But although the rabbi asks us to give before Yom Kippur, no money changes hands on the day of Yom Kippur itself.

Yosef says:
Yom Kippur is our holiest day of the year. We fast for 25 hours. My father goes to the synagogue early in the morning and stays there all day.

Many Jews who live in Israel go to pray at the Western Wall at Yom Kippur. The Western Wall is a very important place for the Jewish people. It is the only remaining part of the Second Temple, the place of worship that was built about 2,500 years ago but was destroyed by the Romans in 70 CE. Many people think it is right to go to this very holy place on the holiest day of the year.

Saul says:
Yom Kippur, like Shabbat, is a holy day, and we are not allowed to use money on this solemn day.

Leah says:
At Yom Kippur there are five different services over the course of the holiday. The holiday begins an hour before sunset and finishes about an hour after sunset the next day.

▲ *People begin to gather at the Western Wall in Jerusalem at Yom Kippur.*

A Favourite Festival
Leah's story

One of my favourite holidays is Chanukah. It celebrates the end of a terrible time in Jewish history. The Jews had been ruled by the Greeks, who had tried to stop them practising their religion, ruined the Temple in Jerusalem, and tried to make them eat pork, torturing those who refused. The Jews fought the Greeks and won. They then restored the Temple and dedicated it **again.**

Saul says:
As we light the candles we sing a blessing. Then when the candles are lit we sing the song *Maoz Tzur* (Rock of Ages).

I use the candle ▶ *called the shamash to light the eight other candles for Chanukah (see opposite).*

22

The miracle of the oil

When they rededicated the Temple, the Jews had only enough holy oil for the Temple light to burn for one night. But a miracle happened and this tiny amount of oil lasted for eight days, giving them time to make some more. This is why we eat foods made with oil at Chanukah – latkes (potato pancakes) and sufganiot (jam doughnuts).

Chanukah candles

At Chanukah we light candles every evening of the eight-day festival. The candles are put in a menorah, which has eight candle-holders and a ninth for the shamash, the candle that we use to light the other candles. On the first night of the festival we light one candle, and then light another one each evening until they are all lit. We also say blessings and sing Chanukah songs.

The dreidel

I like playing dreidel at Chanukah. The dreidel is a spinning top with four sides. Each side has a letter, Nun, Gimel, Hay, and Shin (standing for "Nes gadol haya sham", "A great miracle happened there").

◄ *We play dreidel, winning fake chocolate money, which we then eat.*

A New Baby
Leah's story

When a Jewish baby boy is eight days old there is a very special ceremony. The ceremony is called the Brit Milah and it involves cutting a tiny piece from the baby's foreskin – this is called circumcision. This has been done to Jewish boys for thousands of years as a clear sign that they are Jewish.

A sign of the covenant

Brit Milah is carried out because of a promise that was made between Abraham and God, and which is described in the Torah. In the Torah, God commands Abraham to circumcise himself and his descendents as a symbol of His covenant with the Jewish people, in which God chose the Jews to be a "light to the other nations".

▼ *This is Jeremy's Brit Milah. In order from left to right: the mohel, my baby brother Jeremy, the sandek (sitting) and my father.*

The sandek

When a boy is circumcised, he is held still by an honoured person. This person, called the sandek, may be one of the baby's grandfathers, a rabbi, or a family friend. When my youngest brother Jeremy had his Brit Milah ceremony, the sandek was my great uncle. The ceremony was carried out by a mohel, a Jewish adult who has been specially trained.

At School
Kelly's story

▲ Behind me is a poster showing the Hebrew letters.

▲ The children are reading from their Jewish studies books. They are learning about the festival of Tu Bishvat – the birthday of the trees.

I go to King David Primary School in Victory Park, Johannesburg. King David School is a Jewish school, so as well as doing ordinary school subjects, we learn Hebrew and do Jewish studies too.

Learning Hebrew
I think it is important to learn Hebrew so that I can read the Torah and the other parts of the Hebrew Bible, and understand prayers, songs, and blessings in the language. In Jewish studies we learn about the history of our people, about life in Israel, and about other issues that affect Jewish people.

Other subjects
Our other school subjects include the South African language Afrikaans, and we might soon do another African language, Zulu, as well. I am good at Maths but my favourite subjects are Afrikaans and Art. I am in the athletics and cross-country running teams at school. I also enjoy ballet, which I do after school.

Coming of Age
Kelly's story

▲ *Me and my school friends Shayna and Abigail. When I am 12 I will have a coming-of-age ceremony called a Bat Mitzvah.*

My brother Dean is 13 years old and has just "come of age". This means he is now old enough to take on the responsibilities of an adult in the Jewish community. A ceremony called a Bar Mitzvah marks the time when a boy comes of age.

Bar Mitzvah and Bat Mitzvah

The phrase "Bar Mitzvah" means "Son of the Commandment". In other words, Dean's Bar Mitzvah shows that he is a full member of the family of the Jewish people. He is old enough to be counted as one of the ten people needed for a service in the synagogue. When I am 12 I will have a similar coming-of-age ceremony called a "Bat Mitzvah" ("Daughter of the Commandment").

26

Saul says:
Before your Bar Mitzvah, you study the Torah and learn how to sing it. You also learn all about what it means to be Jewish.

Preparation

To prepare for his Bar Mitzvah, Dean had to learn the special singing notes (called the Trope) used for the week's portion of the Torah. He also learned all about the meaning of becoming Bar Mitzvah.

▲ *This is my brother Dean reading from the Torah before his Bar Mitzvah.*

The ceremony

The ceremony took place at the synagogue. Dean chanted the week's portion of the Torah and gave a talk about it. After the ceremony, we had a party, when lots of family members and friends came to celebrate the joyous occasion and to give presents to Dean.

Leah says:
As I am eight years old I have not had my Bat Mitzvah yet. I look forward to celebrating it in four years' time.

◄ *Leah's sister Rebecca reads the Torah practising for her Bat Mitzvah ceremony.*

Glossary

ancestry Family members from the distant past.

capital The main city of a country or state.

chew the cud The way in which cows and similar animals eat by bring up food from their stomachs and chewing it again.

Chumash The Hebrew name for the Torah, the first five books of the Hebrew Bible.

commandments Instructions, especially those given to people by God.

commemorate To mark the memory of a person or a past event with a ceremony or holy day.

dedicated To set a religious building apart as a place for the worship of God.

diligently Carefully and with much effort or hard work.

festivals Days that have special religious importance and are marked by celebration.

forbidden Not allowed.

foreskin The loose fold of skin covering the upper part of a penis.

Gemorah Books containing discussions of the Mishnah; together Mishnah and Gemorah make up the collection called the Talmud.

Hebrew The language spoken by the early Jews and still in modern Israel, and in which the scriptures are written.

inscribe To write or carve letters.

kippah A close-fitting, brimless cap worn by many male Jews.

matzah A type of bread, made without yeast, eaten on Passover.

meaningful A term used to describe something that has special meaning or purpose.

Mishnah Collection of discussions of the Torah by early rabbis.

parchment A material made from the skin of sheep or goats and used for writing on.

recite To repeat out loud.

repent To feel sorry for bad things you have done in the past and to give up sinful ways in the future.

revere To feel special love, respect, or devotion towards someone, especially towards God.

scribe A person who has been trained to write out texts, especially the text of the Torah.

scripture Religious writing, especially the Torah and the Hebrew Bible as a whole.

Second Temple Centre of Jewish worship in Jerusalem, built in 516 BCE and destroyed in 70 CE.

slaughtered Killed.

Sukkot The seven-day festival marking the time the Jews wandered in the desert after the end of their time in Egypt.

synagogue The Jewish place of worship and religious instruction.

Torah The first five books of the Hebrew Bible, believed to contain the words of God as passed to the great Jewish leader Moses.

Further Information

Books
Judaism
Douglas Charing (Dorling Kindersley, 2003)

The Jewish World
Douglas Charing (Hodder Wayland, 2001)

Jewish Festivals Through the Year
Anita Ganeri (Franklin Watts, 2003)

Judaism Around the World (Atlas of World Faiths)
Cath Senker, (Franklin Watts, 2007)

Websites
BBC Religion and Ethics
www.bbc.co.uk/religion/religions/judaism

Jewish Children's Learning Network
www.akhlah.com

Judaism 101
www.jewfaq.org/index.htm

Religion facts
www.religionfacts.com/judaism/fastfacts/overview.htm

Note to parents and teachers: Every effort has been made by the Publishers to ensure that these websites are suitable for children, that they are of the highest educational value, and that they contain no inappropriate or offensive material. However, because of the nature of the Internet, it is impossible to guarantee that the contents of these sites will not be altered. We advise that Internet access is supervised by a responsible adult.

The Jewish Year

Because the Jewish calendar works in a different way from the western one, Jewish festivals and High Holy Days occur on different days and different months of the western calendar each year. In this list of important days in the Jewish year, the name of the Jewish month when each day falls is followed by the western months in which it usually occurs.

The Jewish calendar begins with Rosh Hashanah, the Jewish New Year, which begins a ten-day period during which Jews ask forgiveness for their sins, ending on Yom Kippur, the solemn Day of Atonement. Other festivals commemorate key events in the history of the Jews.

Rosh Hashanah
The Jewish New Year festival.
Tishri (September/October)

Yom Kippur

The Day of Atonement, the solemn day when Jewish people **repent** their sins.
Tishri (September/October)

Sukkot

The days commemorating the time that the Jews spent in the desert on their journey to the Promised Land.
Tishri (September/October)

Simchat Torah

A celebration giving thanks for the Torah, following the end of Sukkot.
Tishri (September/October)

Chanukah

The festival of lights commemorating the rededication of the temple in Jerusalem after a period when the Holy Land had been occupied by foreign rulers.
Kislev (December)

Purim

A joyful festival that marks the time when Jewish heroine Esther saved her people from being wiped out.
Adar (March)

Pesach

Passover – the festival that celebrates the Jews' escape from persecution in Egypt.
Nisan (March/April)

Shavuot

A festival that commemorates the time when Moses received the Torah on Mount Sinai.
Sivan (May/June)

Index